FAVORITE MEAT DISHES

CONTENTS

MEAT DISHES FROM AROUND THE WORLD

In every country of the world, meat is prepared in a variety of delicious ways. We'll show you some of the best and easiest recipes that your family and guests will love.

THE MEDITERRANEAN

An enticing aroma of fresh herbs and spices fills the kitchens of this region, where the best meat is marinated and browned in the finest olive oil. One of Italy's world-famous dishes is Saltimbocca alla Romana, which is prepared with thin slices of veal, prosciutto, and sage.

NORTH AMERICA

In the United States, the influence of many generations of home cooks who immigrated from around the world—including from neighboring Mexico—is delectably apparent in the national cuisine. It's a tempting feast of flavors—from juicy hamburgers to Cajun blackened steak.

NORTHERN & EASTERN EUROPE

In times past, meat was considered a luxury, the crowning touch to lavish 12-course repasts served at castles and in the homes of aristocrats. Today we can enjoy meat in our everyday meals. The cuisine of Northern and Eastern Europe offers a wealth of beef, veal, pork, and

4

ASIA & THE FAR EAST

Tender meat and crispy vegetables are sliced or cubed, then flashed in a hot wok. The colorful, tasty result is a mainstay of Asian cuisine.

Using soy sauce, sweet-and-sour marinades, coconut milk, and other tantalizing flavors, cooks of this part of the world conjure up scintillating dishes.

LATIN AMERICA

Tamales stuffed with various combinations of fillings—refined marriages of meats, fruits, and fresh vegetables—make for one of the vibrant dishes that are the pride of this vast territory.

lamb dishes. In the country kitchens of this large, ethnically diverse region, some of the world's undeniable classics have been developed. These favorites—including steak frites, Wiener schnitzel, and beef Stroganoff—are as rich and varied as the people who prepare and delight in them.

STEAK ALLA PIZZAIOLA

ITALY

Here, juicy steaks are served with pizzaiola, a zesty Neapolitan tomato sauce seasoned with garlic and oregano. It's full of family-pleasing flavors—and easy to cook, too!

INGREDIENTS
(Serves 4)

- 2 pounds plum tomatoes
- 1 large onion
- 3 garlic cloves
- ¼ cup olive oil
- ½ teaspoon *each* salt and pepper
- 2 teaspoons fresh oregano or 1 teaspoon dried
- 4 top round steaks (6 ounces each)
- ¼ cup fresh basil, plus sprigs

INGREDIENT TIP

Fresh oval plum tomatoes are meaty and delicious. You should have no trouble finding this popular variety at the market or a fruit-and-vegetable stand. Otherwise, you can substitute 35 ounces of canned peeled tomatoes.

1 Bring a large saucepan of water to a boil. Add the tomatoes in batches and blanch for 1 minute. With a slotted spoon, transfer them to a bowl of ice water. Peel and quarter the tomatoes.

2 Peel and chop the onion. Peel the garlic and cut into paper-thin slices. In a deep skillet, heat 2 tablespoons of the oil over low heat. Add the onion and garlic and cook gently, stirring often, until softened.

3 Add the tomatoes, salt, pepper, and oregano. Bring to a simmer. Continue to cook for 20 minutes until the tomatoes have broken down and the sauce is thickened.

4 Heat the remaining 2 tablespoons oil in a large skillet over medium-high heat. Season the steaks with salt and pepper and add to the pan. Cook for about 5 minutes, turning once, for medium-rare.

5 Finely chop the basil; stir into the tomato sauce. Season the sauce and serve with the steak. Garnish with basil sprigs.

Step 3

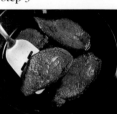

Step 4

Step 5

Preparation: 20 minutes
Cooking: 30 minutes
Per serving: 455 cal; 37 g pro; 27 g fat; 16 g carb.

TYPICALLY NEAPOLITAN

A meal without tomatoes is almost unimaginable in Naples. The Neapolitans have a great variety of tomato sauces, of which pizzaiola is a sumptuous garlicky favorite, served over everything from pasta to pizza to meats.

COOKING TIP

You can prepare the tomato sauce in advance. If it is well covered, a tomato sauce will keep in the refrigerator for 4–5 days or in the freezer for over 6 months. If you use precooked pizzaiola sauce, simply heat it while the meat is cooking.

SERVING TIPS

Mixed vegetables, such as artichoke hearts and broccoli, go great with this entree.

 Try an Italian red wine, such as a full-bodied Chianti, with this dish.

VEAL SALTIMBOCCA

"Saltimbocca," the name of this Roman dish, means "jump into my mouth." And that's no wonder—for these little bundles of tender veal, prosciutto, and sage are absolutely delicious!

INGREDIENTS

(Serves 4)

- 1 pound veal cutlets
- 4 ounces (8 slices) prosciutto ham, sliced paper-thin (see Ingredient Tip)
- 16 fresh sage leaves
- 3 tablespoons flour
- salt and pepper
- 1 stick butter
- 2 tablespoons vegetable oil
- ½ cup chicken or beef broth
- ¼ cup dry white wine

INGREDIENT TIP

In Italy, there are many kinds of air-dried, cured ham, but prosciutto, the famous ham from Parma, is preferred over all others. For maximum flavor, the slices should be paper-thin.

1 Cut the veal into 8 pieces weighing about 2 ounces each. Pound the veal to about ⅛-inch thickness with a meat mallet or rolling pin. Place 1 slice of ham over each veal slice, then cut in half.

2 Place a sage leaf on each piece of ham and attach with a toothpick. On a plate, mix together the flour, ¼ teaspoon salt, and ⅛ teaspoon pepper. Dip the veal in the mixture to coat on the bottom and shake off any excess flour.

3 Melt 6 tablespoons of the butter in the oil in a large skillet over medium heat. Sauté the veal for 3 minutes on each side, until golden brown. Transfer to a platter, remove the toothpicks, and keep warm.

4 Drain off the fat from the pan. Place the pan over high heat and add the broth and wine. Bring to a boil, stirring constantly to deglaze the pan. Boil until the liquid is reduced by half. Remove the pan from the heat. Whisk in ¼ teaspoon salt, ⅛ teaspoon pepper, and the remaining butter, whisking until the butter melts and the sauce thickens slightly. Serve immediately with the veal.

Step 1

Step 2

Step 3

Preparation: 25 minutes
Cooking: 10 minutes
Per serving: 410 cal; 33 g pro; 27 g fat; 5 g carb.

TYPICALLY ITALIAN

Historically, recipes with veal were not as common in Southern Italy as in the North. This dish from Rome is a rare exception. Veal holds a special place on the Italian menu and is prepared in a variety of styles. Veal dishes from Lombardy, Piedmont, and Liguria each have distinctive local flavors.

COOKING TIPS

• Instead of using veal, you might want to try thin turkey or chicken fillets. The cooking time is approximately the same.

• You can use Marsala, a Sicilian dessert wine, instead of dry white wine, to make the sauce.

SERVING TIPS

Try serving antipasti—sliced meats, marinated vegetables, and olives—before this main course.

 A refreshing Italian white wine, either Frascati or Soave, makes a great complement to this dish.

$\mathscr{F}$LORENTINE MEDALLIONS OF PORK

ITALY

Flavorful and easy to cook, these tender pork medallions are served on a bed of spinach and topped with a creamy cheese sauce—a classic preparation from Florence, Italy.

INGREDIENTS

(Serves 4)

- 4 tablespoons butter
- 4 teaspoons flour
- ¾ cup milk
- ½ cup grated fontina cheese
- ⅔ cup grated Parmesan
- ¼ teaspoon dry mustard
- salt and pepper
- 2 tablespoons olive oil
- 4 boneless pork loin chops (6 ounces each)
- 2 pounds fresh spinach, steamed
- 2 garlic cloves, peeled and finely chopped
- 1 teaspoon fresh rosemary

INGREDIENT TIP

Any mildly tangy semisoft cheese, such as Gruyère or Swiss, can be used instead of the fontina.

1 Melt 2 tablespoons butter in a small saucepan over medium heat. Whisk in the flour; stir for 2 minutes. Gradually whisk in the milk. Bring to a boil, stirring constantly. Remove from the heat; stir in the fontina, half the Parmesan, and the mustard.

2 Season the pork with salt and pepper. In a large skillet, melt the remaining 2 tablespoons butter in the oil over medium heat. Add the pork and cook for 6 minutes, turning once, until golden on both sides. Transfer to a plate and keep warm.

3 Coarsely chop the spinach. Remove all but 1 tablespoon fat from the skillet. Add the garlic and rosemary, and sauté for 2 minutes. Add the spinach; heat through, and spread on an ovenproof platter.

4 Preheat the broiler. Place the pork on the spinach. Cover with the cheese sauce; sprinkle with the remaining Parmesan. Broil 2–3 minutes, until golden brown.

Step 1

Step 2

Step 4

Preparation: 20 minutes
Cooking: 20 minutes
Per serving: 712 cal; 52 g pro; 51 g fat; 13 g carb.

TYPICALLY FLORENTINE

Spinach arrived in Italy from the Middle East during the 17th century and quickly gained popularity not only as a side dish but also as a filling for cakes and pies. The Florentine style of preparing fresh spinach is with cheese and garlic.

COOKING TIP

When cooking fresh spinach to make 4 servings, buy at least 2 pounds. To clean, discard the stems. Soak the leaves in plenty of water. Drain lightly, place in a large pot, and cook over medium heat just until wilted. Note: If time is a problem, two 10-ounce boxes of frozen leaf spinach can be used. Just thaw and gently squeeze the leaves to remove excess water.

SERVING TIPS

Fried potatoes and steamed seasonal vegetables make ideal side dishes here.

An Italian dry white or red wine will go especially well with this dish.

11

ᴀNDALUSIAN PORK

SPAIN

This hearty pork dish of Southern Spain features bright red bell peppers, juicy tomatoes, and crisp green beans. It's topped with a sprinkling of tangy cheese, then broiled to a golden brown.

INGREDIENTS
(Serves 4)

- 1 pound green beans
- 3 large plum tomatoes
- 4 boneless pork loin medallions (6 ounces each)
- salt and black pepper
- 1 large red bell pepper
- 2 garlic cloves
- ¼ cup olive oil
- ½ teaspoon crushed red pepper
- 5 ounces Manchego, Asiago, or aged Gouda cheese

INGREDIENT TIP

Manchego, perhaps the most popular cheese in Spain, is a firm, sharp cheese.

1 Trim the ends of the green beans. In a large saucepan of boiling water, cook the beans for 7 minutes. Remove with a slotted spoon to a colander and rinse with cold water. Place in a 2-quart baking dish. In the same boiling water, blanch the tomatoes, then rinse with cold water. Peel, finely chop, and set aside.

2 Remove any fat or sinew from the meat. Sprinkle with 1 teaspoon salt and ½ teaspoon black pepper. Seed and devein the bell pepper and cut it into thin strips. Peel and mince the garlic.

3 Heat 2 tablespoons oil in a large nonstick skillet over high heat and brown the pork for 3 minutes on each side. Place on top of the green beans. Add the remaining oil to the drippings in the skillet and sauté the pepper strips and garlic over medium-high heat for 5 minutes. Add the crushed pepper and cook for 2 minutes. Spoon on top of the pork.

4 Preheat the oven to 375°F. Grate the cheese and sprinkle on top of the vegetables. Bake until the cheese browns, about 15 minutes.

Step 2

Step 3

Step 4

Preparation: 35 minutes
Cooking: 30 minutes
Per serving: 559 cal; 50 g pro; 32 g fat; 11 g carb.

TYPICALLY ANDALUSIAN

The local culture of Southern Spain is as colorful and lively as the cuisine of this region. In Seville, Granada, Cordoba, and other cities and villages, fiestas spill into the streets and squares, where all can enjoy the vibrant performances of flamenco dancers.

COOKING TIP

When cooking the meat, make sure the heat is not
too high—the outside may brown too quickly, leaving
the inside pink and raw. It is also important to take
the meat out of the refrigerator a little while before
sautéing so that it will cook more evenly.

SERVING TIPS

Try serving a cold vegetable
soup, like the famous gazpacho,
with fresh tomatoes, cucumbers, and peppers.

With your meal, enjoy a robust Spanish red wine,
like Rioja, which is aged in oak casks.

ℒAMB AVGOLEMONO

INGREDIENTS
(Serves 4-5)

- 2 pounds boneless leg of lamb
- 3 tablespoons olive oil
- salt and pepper
- 1 head Romaine lettuce
- 4 scallions
- 1 celery rib
- ½ cup fresh dill sprigs
- 4 fresh parsley sprigs
- 2 eggs
- 1½ teaspoons dried oregano
- 3 tablespoons fresh lemon juice

INGREDIENT TIP

Other seasonal vegetables such as small artichoke hearts or fresh large flat Italian green beans can be used as well. Use ½ pound of each kind of vegetable.

The secret's in the sauce of this hearty Mediterranean favorite. This delicious mixture of savory eggs and tangy lemons is called "avgolemono" in Greek.

1 Dice the lamb into ¾-inch cubes. Heat the oil in a skillet over medium-high heat and fry the meat in 3–4 batches until it's browned on all sides. Return all the meat to the pan. Add 1 cup water, ½ teaspoon salt, and ¼ teaspoon pepper. Bring to a boil. Cover and simmer for 1 hour over low heat.

2 Rinse the lettuce, scallions, and celery, and pat dry. Cut the lettuce into thin strips. Slice the scallions and celery. Finely chop half of the dill; chop the parsley. Add all the vegetables and the chopped dill and parsley to the meat, stir, and cook for 5 minutes. Remove the pan from the heat.

3 Whisk the eggs with the oregano in a medium bowl. Strain the cooking liquid from the lamb into a small bowl. Slowly whisk half the hot liquid into the egg mixture, add the lemon juice, and whisk in the remaining hot cooking liquid. Stir the liquid into the lamb.

4 Heat the lamb over low heat until the sauce thickens. (Do not boil or the eggs will curdle.) Garnish with the remaining dill.

Step 1

Step 2

Step 3

Preparation: 20 minutes
Cooking: 1 hour 5 minutes
Per serving: 547 cal; 37 g pro;
41 g fat; 5 g carb.

TYPICALLY GREEK
The Greeks have always prepared dishes according to the time of year, using seasonal ingredients. Lamb Avgolemono, prepared with fresh herbs, young vegetables, and tender lamb, is a typical springtime dish.

COOKING TIP

The most important thing to consider here is the heating of the eggs for the sauce. Off the heat, add the hot cooking liquid slowly to the eggs in order to "temper" or warm them. As the sauce heats and thickens, stir the mixture constantly over low heat. The mixture should never boil—even after tempering, the eggs will curdle.

SERVING TIPS

Stuffed grape leaves are a delicious appetizer. Serve them with tomato wedges and a squeeze of fresh lemon.

Ouzo, the anise-flavored Greek liqueur, is a splendid aperitif for this dish.

ZESTY MEATBALLS—THREE WAYS

*Here's a variety of delicious and economical recipes for meatballs,
which are enjoyed in many different ways all over the world.*

BASIC RECIPE

(SERVES 4)
- 6 tablespoons dried bread crumbs
- 5 tablespoons milk
- 1 small onion
- 1 pound ground beef or lamb
- 1 egg
- salt and pepper
- ¼ teaspoon allspice
- 2 tablespoons flour
- 2 tablespoons vegetable oil

*Different sauces and seasonings make this basic
recipe especially versatile.*

1 Combine the bread crumbs and milk in a large bowl and let soak for 10 minutes.

2 Finely chop the onion; add to the bread-crumb mixture. Add the ground meat, egg, 1 teaspoon salt, ½ teaspoon pepper, and the allspice. Mix well.

3 Form the mixture into 1-inch balls and dust with the flour. Heat the oil in a large non-stick skillet over low heat and fry the meatballs until browned on all sides and cooked through, 10–15 minutes. Drain on paper towels. Place on a heatproof platter in a warm oven.

MEATBALLS WITH TOMATO-ONION GARNISH

Preparation: 25 minutes   Cooking: 15 minutes

MOROCCO

- 1 cup fresh parsley leaves
- ⅓ cup fresh mint leaves
- Basic Meatballs
- 6 plum tomatoes
- 1 small red onion
- 3 tablespoons olive oil
- salt and pepper
- pita bread
- lemon wedges

4 Place the parsley and mint leaves on a platter and top with the warm meatballs.

5 Quarter the tomatoes and place in a large bowl. Peel the onion, thinly slice crosswise, separate into rings, and add to the tomatoes. Add the oil, 1 teaspoon salt, and ½ teaspoon pepper. Serve with the meatballs. Pass the bread and lemon.

MEATBALLS WITH TOMATO SAUCE

Preparation: 25 minutes   Cooking: 45 minutes

ITALY

- 1 onion
- 2 garlic cloves
- 3 tablespoons olive oil
- 1 can (28 ounces) crushed peeled tomatoes
- salt and pepper
- 1 pound spaghetti
- Basic Meatballs
- 4 sprigs fresh basil

4 Peel the onion and garlic and finely chop. Heat the oil in a large saucepan over medium heat and sauté the onion and garlic for 10 minutes, until soft. Add the tomatoes and cook for 10 minutes. Add ¼ teaspoon *each* salt and pepper.

5 Cook the spaghetti as the label directs. Put the meatballs in the sauce and simmer over low heat for 10 minutes. Serve over the spaghetti, garnished with basil.

MEATBALLS WITH YOGURT-MINT SAUCE

Preparation: 25 minutes   Cooking: 15 minutes

TURKEY

- ½ cucumber
- 8 fresh mint sprigs
- 1 cup plain yogurt
- salt and black pepper
- ¼ teaspoon ground cumin
- ¼ teaspoon cayenne pepper
- 4 rolls or pitas
- Basic Meatballs

4 Peel and finely chop the cucumber and place in a large bowl. Reserve the tops of the mint sprigs; chop the remainder and add to the cucumber. Add the yogurt, ½ teaspoon salt, ¼ teaspoon black pepper, the cumin, and cayenne. Mix well.

5 Split and warm the rolls. Add the meatballs to the yogurt mixture, stir to coat, and spoon into the rolls. Garnish with the mint-sprig tops.

SERVING TIPS French fries and a fresh green salad make excellent accompaniments to the steak.

A full-bodied French red wine will stand up well to the meat—try a Bordeaux.

$\mathcal{S}$TEAK WITH SEASONED BUTTERS

FRANCE

Two butter rosettes lend an elegant touch to this favorite at French bistros. They not only make for an extremely attractive presentation, but also add an extra-special flavor.

INGREDIENTS
(Serves 4)

- 1 stick unsalted butter, softened
- 1 tablespoon prepared horseradish
- ½ teaspoon grainy mustard
- salt and pepper
- 2 ounces blue cheese
- ½ teaspoon finely grated lemon peel
- 4 boneless sirloin steaks (about 6 ounces each)
- 2 tablespoons oil
- 1 tablespoon chopped parsley

INGREDIENT TIP

You can use fresh horseradish in this dish. Peel and finely grate. Place any leftovers in a glass jar. Stir in a bit of white vinegar, cover with a lid, and refrigerate for later use.

1 Line a plate with a sheet of waxed paper. Place half of the butter in a small bowl. Add the horseradish, mustard, ¼ teaspoon salt, and a pinch of pepper and stir until blended. Refrigerate for 15 minutes to firm slightly. Spoon into a small pastry bag with a wide star tip and pipe out 4 rosettes with the butter on the paper-lined plate.

Step 1

2 Place the remaining butter in another bowl. Add the blue cheese, lemon peel, and a pinch *each* of salt and pepper and mix well. Refrigerate for 15 minutes to firm slightly. Spoon into the pastry bag and pipe another 4 rosettes onto the same plate. Freeze while you prepare the steaks.

Step 3

3 Season the meat with ¼ teaspoon salt and ⅛ teaspoon pepper. Heat the oil in a large skillet over medium heat. Add the steaks and cook for 4 minutes, turning once, for medium-rare, 6 minutes for medium and 8 minutes for well done.

4 Put the steaks on individual serving plates, then place a rosette of each butter on top. Sprinkle with the parsley and serve.

Step 3

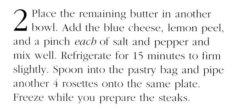

Preparation: 45 minutes
Cooking: 10 minutes
Per serving: 661 cal; 36 g pro; 57 g fat; 1 g carb.

TYPICALLY FRENCH
The French bistro is a cozy place where hearty, tempting fare abounds. One of the most typical dishes to be found in a bistro—from Normandy to Provence—is steak frites, or steak with french fries.

STEAK AU POIVRE

FRANCE

INGREDIENTS
(Serves 4)

- 1½ teaspoons black peppercorns
- 4 filets mignons or boneless sirloins (8 ounces each)
- salt
- 4 shallots
- 2 tablespoons butter
- 1 tablespoon oil
- 1 tablespoon drained green peppercorns
- ¼ cup cognac or brandy
- ½ cup beef broth

INGREDIENT TIP

Whole green peppercorns are the soft, underripe version of the berries that are grown and processed to make store-bought ground pepper (a spray is shown in the photo at right). Usually preserved in brine, their flavor is milder than black or white peppercorns.

This classic French entree is just right for special occasions—a perfectly cooked steak, crusty on the outside and juicy on the inside, smothered in a spicy pepper sauce. Who can resist?

1 Coarsely crush the black peppercorns in a mortar with a pestle or on a board with a rolling pin. Press both sides of each steak into the pepper, then sprinkle with ¼ teaspoon salt. Peel and chop the shallots.

2 Melt 1 tablespoon butter in the oil in a large skillet over medium-high heat. Add the steaks. For medium-rare, cook fillets for 8–10 minutes, turning once, and cook boneless sirloins for 6 minutes, turning once. Transfer the steaks to individual serving plates and cover to keep warm.

3 Pour off all but 1 tablespoon fat from the pan. Add the shallots and cook over medium-low heat until soft, about 5 minutes, stirring often. Add the green peppercorns and the cognac. Bring to a boil over high heat, then add the broth. Cook until the liquid is reduced by half, about 3 minutes.

4 Remove the pan from the heat and add the remaining 1 tablespoon butter, whisking until the butter melts and the sauce is smooth. Season the sauce to taste, then spoon over each steak and serve.

Step 1

Step 2

Step 4

Preparation: 15 minutes
Cooking: 20 minutes
Per serving: 751 cal; 41 g pro; 61 g fat; 2 g carb.

TYPICALLY PARISIAN

Parisians will go to great lengths to find the highest-quality cuts of meat. It's not uncommon for gourmands to travel to the other end of town to an esteemed *boucher* (butcher) in order to purchase a first-rate steak.

COOKING TIPS

• Take care to purchase the best meat available. Look for beef with an ample marbling of fat throughout, which makes for a juicy, delicious steak.
• Before cooking the steak, wrap the sides with kitchen string to give the meat a uniform thickness and help it cook evenly.

SERVING TIPS

Roasted or boiled new potatoes, along with a fresh mixed salad, make tasty accompaniments here.

A full-bodied Bordeaux or Burgundy is an appropriate wine pairing for this meal.

NORMAN PORK CUTLETS

FRANCE

In this recipe, tender pork cutlets are briefly pan-seared, then simmered in a sauce that hails from Normandy—a luscious blend of fresh cream and tangy cider, plus a hint of tarragon.

INGREDIENTS

(Serves 4)

- 3 shallots
- 4 rib end pork chops (8 ounces each)
- salt and pepper
- 2 tablespoons olive oil
- 1 cup hard cider
- ⅔ cup heavy cream
- 2 tablespoons chopped fresh tarragon

INGREDIENT TIP

Hard cider—which is dry, not sweet—is a favorite drink in Normandy. The best cider is produced in Vallée d'Auge in the Calvados region, which also produces a fiery brandy of the same name. If you can't find hard cider, you can substitute a dry white wine.

1 Peel and finely chop the shallots, then set aside. Season the pork chops with ¼ teaspoon salt and ⅛ teaspoon pepper.

2 Heat the oil in a large skillet over medium-high heat. Add the chops and cook until browned on both sides, about 6 minutes. (The chops will not be cooked through.) Transfer to a plate and cover to keep warm.

3 Remove all but 1 tablespoon fat from the pan. Add the shallots and cook over medium-low heat, stirring occasionally, until golden and softened, about 5 minutes. Add the cider and bring to a boil. Simmer until reduced by half, about 7 minutes. Add the cream and tarragon.

4 Return the chops to the skillet. Cover, reduce the heat to low, and simmer gently for 10 minutes, turning the chops once or twice.

5 Place the chops on individual dinner plates. Season the sauce with salt and pepper, and spoon over the chops.

Step 1

Step 2

Step 3

Preparation: 15 minutes
Cooking: 35 minutes
Per serving: 485 cal; 31 g pro; 38 g fat; 3 g carb.

TYPICALLY NORMAN

The people of Normandy harvest an abundance of vegetables and fruits from the green fields and huge orchards that characterize the region. The apple plays an important role in the local cuisine.

COOKING TIPS

• For a variation, you can stir a little grainy mustard into the finished sauce before seasoning it with the salt and pepper.

• If there seems to be too much fat in the pan after cooking the chops, carefully pour out all but 1 tablespoon before adding the cider for the sauce.

SERVING TIPS

Egg noodles and fresh vegetables or a mixed salad make a great complement to the pork.

 With your meal, enjoy a glass of dry cider or a full-bodied Chardonnay.

VEAL-AND-MUSHROOM ROULADES

FRANCE

"Roulades" are thin cuts of meat rolled around a savory filling—here, sliced veal encloses a delicious stuffing. A sauce of wine and mushrooms adds a delectable touch to this dish.

INGREDIENTS
(Serves 4)

- 1 ounce dried cèpe, or porcini, mushrooms
- 4 thin veal cutlets (about 4 ounces each)
- salt and white pepper
- 2 shallots
- 3 garlic cloves
- 6 ounces ground veal
- ¼ cup chopped parsley
- 4 thin slices bacon
- 1 tablespoon butter
- 1 tablespoon vegetable oil
- 1 carrot
- 1 celery rib
- ½ cup beef broth
- ½ cup dry white wine
- ½ cup heavy cream
- parsley sprigs for garnish

INGREDIENT TIP

The liquid from soaking the dried mushrooms can be used in addition to broth or as a substitute for part of the liquid called for in the recipe.

1 Soak the mushrooms in ¾ cup warm water in a small bowl. With a meat mallet or rolling pin, pound the meat to ⅛-inch thickness. Sprinkle with ½ teaspoon salt and ⅛ teaspoon white pepper.

2 Peel the shallots and garlic, finely chop, and place in a medium bowl. Add the ground veal, parsley, ½ teaspoon salt, and ⅛ teaspoon white pepper, and mix well.

3 Spread the stuffing over the veal. Roll up the cutlets and wrap with bacon; secure with toothpicks. Melt the butter in the oil in a large skillet. Brown the roulades over medium-high heat, about 8 minutes.

4 Peel and chop the carrot. Chop the celery. Add the carrot, celery, mushrooms, strained mushroom liquid, broth, and wine to the veal. Bring to a boil. Cover and simmer for 40 minutes over medium heat, turning the roulades every 10 minutes. Remove the roulades and keep warm.

5 Simmer the liquid until reduced by half, about 7 minutes. Stir in the cream and heat through. Serve the sauce with the roulades. Garnish with parsley sprigs.

Step 2

Step 3

Step 4

Preparation: 35 minutes
Cooking: 1 hour
Per serving: 511 cal; 37 g pro; 35 g fat; 8 g carb.

TYPICALLY PÉRIGORD

Périgord, a picturesque region of rolling countryside and lovely villages in the South of France, is famous for its harvests of black truffles and other fine mushrooms. Pigs and dogs are used to sniff out these underground treasures.

COOKING TIP

You should soak the dried mushrooms for 30 minutes to reconstitute them (Step 1). Then scoop them out with a slotted spoon and strain the mushroom liquid in a fine-mesh sieve to remove any grit.

SERVING TIPS

As an appetizer, try foie gras paté, the famous goose liver spread of Périgord, with crisp toast triangles.

 A dry white wine, such as a Graves or Sauvignon Blanc will go well with this meal.

SERVING TIPS A mixed green salad, along with bread or mashed potatoes, complements the dish.

 The perfect refreshment for this repast: a glass of Riesling wine or a cold beer.

SAVORY CROQUETTES WITH MUSHROOM SAUCE

GERMANY

Nothing satisfies like a meat-and-potatoes meal. These hearty yet elegant croquettes, which rank high among Germany's favorite comfort foods, are quick and easy to prepare.

INGREDIENTS
(Serves 4)

- 1 ounce dried cèpe, or porcini, mushrooms
- 1 large baking potato
- 1 medium onion
- 3 garlic cloves
- 3 tablespoons butter
- 1 pound lean ground pork
- salt and pepper
- ½ cup dry white wine
- 1 large egg
- 4 ounces fresh mushrooms
- 1 teaspoon dried thyme
- ¼ cup sour cream

IN ADDITION
- chopped parsley for garnish

INGREDIENT TIP

You can substitute another kind of ground meat in these croquettes. Both ground veal and turkey would work well.

1 Soak dried mushrooms in ½ cup boiling water. Meanwhile, peel and quarter the potato. Place in a small saucepan with water to cover. Simmer until tender, about 20 minutes. Drain; mash the potato; let cool.

2 Peel the onion and garlic; finely chop. Place in a large skillet with 2 tablespoons butter. Cook over low heat until soft. Set half aside on a plate. Add the remaining half to the pork in a bowl. Add ½ teaspoon salt, ¼ teaspoon pepper, and 2 tablespoons of the wine. Add the potato and egg and mix well. Form into 12 patties.

3 Wipe out the skillet, add the remaining 1 tablespoon butter, and place over medium heat. Add the patties; cook on each side for 4 minutes. Transfer to plates; keep warm.

4 Slice the fresh mushrooms. Add to skillet with the thyme and reserved onion mixture; cook for 5 minutes. Add the dried mushrooms, strained soaking liquid, and remaining wine. Boil briskly for 5 minutes.

5 Stir in the sour cream. Season to taste and cook until heated through. Spoon the sauce over the patties; sprinkle with parsley.

Step 2

Step 4

Step 5

Preparation: 25 minutes
Cooking: 20 minutes
Each serving: 402 cal; 27 g pro; 22 g fat; 19 g carb.

TYPICALLY GERMAN
On a cold afternoon, the lush forests of Germany are the place to be for avid mushroom hunters. The tender delicacies are featured in dishes such as these croquettes, which are also known as "rissoles."

$\mathscr{V}$EAL SCALLOPS IN RASPBERRY-CREAM SAUCE

SWITZERLAND

Here, tender veal scallops are smothered in a fragrant, sumptuous sauce made with cream and white wine. Raspberries lend a vibrant touch to this classic Swiss dish.

INGREDIENTS

(Serves 4)

- 1½-pound piece veal tenderloin
- salt and white pepper
- 1 small red onion
- 4 tablespoons butter
- ½ cup dry white wine
- ½ cup heavy cream
- 1 tablespoon raspberry vinegar
- freshly grated nutmeg
- ⅓ cup fresh or frozen raspberries

INGREDIENT TIP

Raspberry vinegar adds a special touch to this dish. If you don't have any, you can use balsamic vinegar or red wine vinegar. Most supermarkets carry an assortment of flavored varieties.

1 Place the veal on a cutting board. With a large sharp knife, thinly slice the meat against the grain into scallops.

2 Season the veal slices lightly with salt and white pepper. Peel the red onion, then very finely chop.

3 Melt the butter in a large wok or skillet over medium-high heat. Add the veal slices and cook for 6 minutes, turning once. Remove the veal to a plate. Add the onion to the pan and cook for 3 minutes.

4 Pour in the wine and cook over high heat until the liquid is reduced by half. Pour in the heavy cream and vinegar. Bring to a simmer and cook until thickened slightly, about 4 minutes. Return the veal to the skillet; cook until heated through.

5 Season to taste with salt, white pepper, and nutmeg. Sprinkle the raspberries on top. Serve the veal immediately.

Step 1

Step 4

Step 5

Preparation: 20 minutes
Cooking: 25 minutes
Per serving: 419 cal; 36 g pro;
28 g fat; 5 g carb.

TYPICALLY SWISS

The idyllic mountain villages of the Swiss Alps are world-famous for their dairy products. The veal that is grown in this region is also of a particularly high quality. With these fine foods readily available, the Swiss have developed wonderful recipes with which to enjoy them.

COOKING TIP

The wok hails from China, not Switzerland, but it allows one to brown meat and onions quickly and evenly and is therefore ideally suitable for the preparation of this Swiss dish. If you do not own a wok, you can use a cast-iron skillet or stainless steel pan instead.

SERVING TIP

Rösti, the Swiss potato pancakes, make an ideal side dish. Offer Swiss cheese and fruit for dessert.

 Swiss white wine, such as a Fendant, or cider, are good beverage choices here.

CLASSIC WIENER SCHNITZEL

AUSTRIA

This mouthwatering favorite from Austria features juicy, tender veal scallopini crusted with golden bread crumbs. Be sure to serve lemon wedges alongside to spritz the browned cutlets.

INGREDIENTS

(Serves 4)

- 2 lemons
- 1 pound veal scallopini, pounded
- 3 tablespoons flour
- salt and pepper
- 1 large egg
- 1 cup plain bread crumbs
- 3 tablespoons butter

IN ADDITION

- finely chopped parsley for garnish

INGREDIENT TIP

For Wiener schnitzel, use veal that's no thicker than ⅛ of an inch. If you need thinner cutlets, place on a cutting board and pound, stroking outward, with a hammerlike or flat round meat tenderizer.

1 Squeeze one of the lemons into a resealable plastic bag. Add the veal to the bag, seal, and then let the meat marinate for 30 minutes.

2 On a plate, toss together the flour, ½ teaspoon salt, and ¼ teaspoon pepper. In a small bowl, whisk the egg with 2 teaspoons cold water. Place the bread crumbs in a shallow bowl.

3 Pat the veal dry with paper towels. Working with one piece at a time, dredge the veal in the flour, then turn in the beaten egg. Coat well with bread crumbs. Set aside.

4 Melt half of the butter in a large skillet over medium-high heat. Fry the veal in batches without crowding until nicely browned, about 4 minutes, turning once. Drain on paper towels and keep warm in a low oven. Repeat with the remaining veal and butter.

5 Slice the second lemon into 8 wedges; turn each in the chopped parsley. Serve lemon wedges with the schnitzel.

Step 3

Step 4

Step 5

Preparation: 15 minutes
Marinating: 30 minutes
Cooking: 4 minutes per batch
Per serving: 352 cal; 30 g pro;
13 g fat; 28 g carb.

TYPICALLY VIENNESE

In earlier times, hot entrees were served all day long in the elegant, beautifully decorated restaurants of Vienna. Wiener schnitzel can be found, to this day, on the menu of almost every restaurant in town. Austrians love to make this easy-to-cook dish at home, too.

COOKING TIP

To keep the first batch of Wiener schnitzel warm, put the cutlets on a baking sheet in a single layer, then place in a low oven for 10 minutes.

SERVING TIPS

Offer side dishes of hearty roasted potatoes and red onion salad with a creamy dressing.

 An Austrian or German beer, or a white Burgundy, tastes delicious with this dish.

SERVING TIPS With the main course, offer wide egg noodles, red beet salad, sour cream, and bread.

A red wine that is not too acidic, such as a well-rounded Burgundy, is a nice pairing.

32

BEEF STROGANOFF

RUSSIA

In this uncomplicated, world-renowned culinary classic, a delectable cream sauce lightly coats tender slices of beef and golden sauteed onions and mushrooms.

INGREDIENTS
(Serves 4)

- 1 pound beef tenderloin
- salt and pepper
- 1 medium onion
- 8 ounces fresh mushrooms
- 2 tablespoons oil
- 3 tablespoons butter
- 1 tablespoon flour
- 1 cup beef broth
- 1 cup sour cream
- 1 tablespoon tomato paste
- 1 teaspoon red wine vinegar
- ½ teaspoon dry mustard

INGREDIENT TIP

As an alternative to fairly pricey beef fillet, you can use budget-savvy top round for this flavorful entree.

1 Thinly slice the beef, then cut into finger-length strips. Season with salt and pepper and set aside. Peel the onion and finely chop. Thinly slice the mushrooms.

2 Heat half of the oil and butter in a large skillet over medium-high heat. Add the meat and cook, stirring, until browned, about 2 minutes. Transfer meat to a plate with tongs.

Step 2

3 Add the remaining oil and butter to the pan. Add the onion; stir for 2 minutes. Add the mushrooms and cook for 5 minutes. Transfer to the plate with the meat.

4 Add the flour to the skillet and stir until nicely browned. Gradually whisk in the broth. Keep stirring until hot and thickened.

Step 3

5 Stir in the sour cream, tomato paste, vinegar, and mustard. Return the mushrooms and meat to the pan; cook until heated through. Season the sauce and serve.

Step 5

Preparation: 20 minutes
Cooking: 25 minutes
Per serving: 488 cal; 28 g pro;
37 g fat; 11 g carb.

TYPICALLY RUSSIAN

This recipe was invented by a French cook for the Russian Prince Stroganoff toward the end of the 19th century. The Stroganoffs became rich through the Siberian fur trade and kept a French chef at each of their many country residences.

GREAT STEAKS—THREE WAYS

Even steak lovers like variety on their plates. Here's our basic recipe,
plus a handful of ideas for delicious sauces you can make in a snap.

BASIC RECIPE

(SERVES 4)
- 4 boneless sirloin steaks or fillet mignon (6–8 ounces each)
- salt and pepper
- 1 tablespoon *each* butter and oil

Follow Steps 1 and 2 to make perfect steak.
Then continue with any Step 3 for a tasty sauce.

1 Remove the steaks from the refrigerator 1 hour before cooking. Season the meat on both sides with salt and pepper.

2 In a large heavy skillet, melt the butter in the oil over medium-high heat. When the butter begins to sizzle, add the steaks. For medium-rare, cook ¾-inch-thick sirloins for about 4 minutes, turning once; cook 1-inch-thick fillets for about 5 minutes. Add 1–2 minutes cooking for medium. Let steaks rest for about 5 minutes before serving.

STEAK WITH SPICY MUSHROOM SAUCE

Preparation: 5 minutes   Cooking: 15 minutes

AUSTRIA

- 4 panfried steaks
- 8 ounces sliced mushrooms
- ¼ cup plus 2 tablespoons dry white wine
- ¾ cup sour cream
- 1½ tablespoons tomato paste
- 1 teaspoon paprika
- fresh thyme leaves for garnish

3 While the steaks are resting, add the mushrooms to the pan and cook for 2 minutes. Pour in the wine and bring to a boil. Continue to cook, stirring, until the liquid is reduced by half, about 4 minutes.

4 Stir in the sour cream, tomato paste, and paprika. Gently heat through. Season to taste; spoon over the steaks. Garnish with the thyme.

STEAK WITH RED WINE AND SHALLOTS

Preparation: 5 minutes   Cooking: 20 minutes

FRANCE

- 4 panfried steaks
- 2 tablespoons butter
- 4 shallots, sliced
- 1 garlic clove, finely chopped
- 1½ cups red wine
- 3 tablespoons chopped parsley

3 While the steaks are resting, melt the butter in the skillet.

4 Add the shallots and garlic and cook over medium-low heat, stirring often, until tender, about 6 minutes.

5 Pour in the wine and bring to a boil. Cook until reduced by half. Stir in the parsley. Season to taste, then spoon the sauce over the steaks.

BARBECUE-STYLE STEAK

Preparation: 5 minutes   Cooking: 10 minutes

USA

- 4 panfried steaks
- 1 green bell pepper, diced
- 1 red onion, sliced
- 1 hot red chile, thinly sliced
- 2 garlic cloves, minced
- 2 tablespoons tomato paste
- 2 tablespoons cider vinegar
- 1-2 tablespoons Worcestershire sauce
- 2 teaspoons light brown sugar

3 While the steaks are resting, put the bell pepper, onion, chile, and garlic in the skillet. Cook over medium heat, stirring, until crisp-tender, about 2 minutes.

4 Add the tomato paste, cider vinegar, Worcestershire sauce, brown sugar, and ½ cup water.

5 Bring to a boil, stirring occasionally. Cook for 1 minute longer. Season to taste, then spoon the sauce over the steaks.

STIR-FRIED BEEF & VEGETABLES

CHINA

Asian cooks know that nothing beats the wok for fragrant, flavorful results—fast! In this indispensable pan, strips of meat cook beautifully, and vegetables remain fresh and crunchy.

INGREDIENTS
(Serves 4)

- 1 pound beef tenderloin
- 2 teaspoons Chinese five spice powder
- ¼ teaspoon black pepper
- 5 tablespoons soy sauce
- 2 bell peppers (1 yellow and 1 green)
- 2 medium carrots
- 4 scallions
- 1 pound plum tomatoes
- 1 can (15 ounces) sliced bamboo shoots
- 1-inch piece fresh ginger
- 3 garlic cloves
- 3 tablespoons oil
- ¼ cup sake or sherry

INGREDIENT TIP

This recipe is also delicious with pork loin, turkey cutlets or boneless chicken breasts. Use 1 pound of your choice.

1 Slice the beef very thin. In a medium bowl, stir the spice powder and black pepper with 3 tablespoons of soy sauce. Add the meat; stir to mix. Set aside for 20 minutes.

2 Halve the bell peppers and seed. Cut into small chunks. Peel the carrots, thinly slice lengthwise, then cut into matchsticks.

Step 2

3 Trim the scallions; slice ½-inch thick. Peel the tomatoes and cut into small chunks. Drain the bamboo shoots in a colander. Peel the ginger and garlic and finely chop.

4 Heat a wok over high heat. Pour in the oil and swirl it around the pan. Stick a wooden spoon into the oil; if bubbles form around the spoon, the oil is ready. Add the meat to the pan and stir-fry for 2 minutes. Transfer with tongs to a wok rack or a plate.

Step 4

5 Add the ginger and garlic to the wok; stir-fry for 1 minute. Add all of the vegetables and stir-fry for 2 minutes. Pour in the sake and the remaining soy sauce. Return the meat to the wok and cook for 2 minutes longer.

Step 5

Preparation: 10 minutes
Marinating: 20 minutes
Cooking: 7 minutes
Per serving: 378 cal; 28 g pro;
20 g fat; 19 g carb.

TYPICALLY CHINESE
Fresh vegetables are adored in Chinese cuisine, which might be what makes it one of the healthiest in the world. On the streets and in the swarming markets, merchants offer a dazzling array of vegetables. The rich supply changes according to season.

COOKING TIPS

• As a rule, heat the wok when it's dry, then add the oil—this ensures even heat and prevents food from sticking. For stirring and mixing, use a long-handled, shovel-like metal spatula (this usually comes with the wok) or any broad, long-handled spoon.

• If you don't have a wok, a large frying pan with a high rim is also suitable.

SERVING TIPS

Use a pretty little Chinese bowl for each serving—and eat with chopsticks. Egg noodles are a wonderful complement.

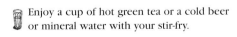 Enjoy a cup of hot green tea or a cold beer or mineral water with your stir-fry.

SERVING TIPS A decoratively peeled orange in the center of the serving dish makes a pretty garnish.

 Green tea served in small porcelain cups elegantly accompanies this colorful, aromatic dish.

PORK WITH SPRING ONIONS

CHINA

It's no wonder that cooks of various nations and cultures have adopted the simple Chinese method of stir-frying, used in this tantalizing pork dish with winning results.

INGREDIENTS
(Serves 4)

- 1 pound boneless pork loin
- 2 garlic cloves
- 3 tablespoons soy sauce
- 3 tablespoons sake or dry sherry
- 1 tablespoon cornstarch
- 1 teaspoon sugar
- salt
- 4 ounces snow peas
- 10 scallions
- 2 tablespoons oil

INGREDIENT TIP

Snow peas are valued in Asian cooking for their crispness and slightly sweet flavor. Carrots have similar traits, and are also suitable for this dish.

1 Thinly slice the pork. Place in a medium bowl. Peel and finely chop the garlic. Add the garlic, soy sauce, sake, cornstarch, sugar, and ½ teaspoon salt to the pork. Mix well and set aside.

2 Cut the snow peas crosswise in half on the diagonal. Trim the root and tough green portion from the scallions and cut the remainder into 1-inch pieces.

3 Preheat the wok over high heat. Add half the oil and the snow peas and stir-fry for 30 seconds. Add the scallions and cook for 1 minute longer. Scrape onto a plate and set aside.

4 Add the remaining 1 tablespoon oil to the wok and swirl to coat the pan. Remove the pork from the marinade, reserving the liquid. Add the meat to the pan and stir-fry for 1 minute. Stir the marinade, then pour into the pan with the meat. Return the vegetables to the wok and stir-fry for 3 minutes, until the sauce is thickened.

Step 1

Step 3

Step 4

Preparation: 20 minutes
Cooking: 10 minutes
Per serving: 344 cal; 25 g pro; 21 g fat; 10 g carb.

TYPICALLY CHINESE

According to ancient Chinese manuscripts, stir-frying has been practiced in China as far back as the 1st century. Suffice it to say that generations of Chinese cooks have had plenty of time to perfect this remarkable technique.

𝒯ANGY CANTONESE PORK

CHINA

This irresistible dish from the city of Canton is a mainstay on Chinese menus and world-famous for its sweet-and-sour flavor. Here's how to make a delicious homemade version.

INGREDIENTS

(Serves 4)

- 1 pound boneless pork loin, trimmed
- 2 garlic cloves
- salt and black pepper
- 1½-inch piece fresh ginger
- 1 small onion
- 1 green bell pepper
- 3 tablespoons fresh orange juice
- 2 tablespoons sugar
- 2 tablespoons rice vinegar or cider vinegar
- 2 tablespoons soy sauce
- 2 tablespoons tomato paste
- 3 tablespoons oil

INGREDIENT TIPS

- Rice vinegar is available in Asian food stores.
- If you wish, use ketchup instead of tomato paste.
- Grate the ginger with, not across, the long fibers.

1 Cut the pork into 1-inch dice and place in a medium bowl. Peel the garlic, place in a small bowl, and mash it with a fork with 1 teaspoon salt. Add the garlic and ¼ teaspoon black pepper to the pork. Peel and grate the ginger, add to the pork, and mix well. Set aside.

2 Peel the onion and cut crosswise into thin slices. Separate the individual onion rings. Cut the bell pepper in half, seed, and devein. Cut into thin slices.

3 Place the orange juice in a small bowl. Stir in the sugar, vinegar, soy sauce, and tomato paste. Stir until the sugar dissolves.

4 Heat a wok over high heat. Add the oil and heat until the oil is hot. Add the meat and stir-fry for 2 minutes. Add the onion rings and bell pepper and stir-fry for 2 minutes. Add the seasoning liquid and stir-fry for 2 minutes. Serve immediately.

Step 1

Step 2

Step 4

Preparation: 35 minutes
Cooking: 8 minutes
Per serving: 314 cal; 26 g pro; 17 g fat; 14 g carb.

TYPICALLY CANTONESE

China's Yangtze River has always played a central role in its people's transportation and trade—introducing new foods and spices to the culture. One such import was the tomato, which the Cantonese use to enhance the sweet, tangy flavor of this dish.

COOKING TIPS

• This dish cooks up in a flash in a wok. So you'll want to have all of the ingredients on hand—rinsed, peeled, and chopped—before you start.

• You can prepare the sauce as much as a day in advance. Keep it covered and refrigerated.

SERVING TIPS

Spring rolls or fried shrimp and steamed or fried rice are great accompaniments.

Serve a semisweet Riesling wine or hot tea, such as jasmine or ginger, with this meal.

SPICY CURRIED BEEF AND BROCCOLI

THAILAND

A heavenly assortment of contrasting tastes—creamy coconut, aromatic ginger and lemongrass, and spicy chile—make this lively Thai dish irresistible.

INGREDIENTS
(Serves 4)

- 1 pound rump steak
- 2 shallots
- 2 garlic cloves
- 1 small red hot chile
- 1½-inch piece fresh ginger
- 1 lime
- 2 stalks lemongrass
- 1 teaspoon ground coriander
- 3 tablespoons soy sauce
- 8 ounces unsweetened grated coconut
- 1 bunch of broccoli
- 3 tablespoons oil

IN ADDITION
- fresh cilantro leaves

INGREDIENT TIP
You'll find fresh or dried lemongrass in Asian food stores. Avoid using powdered lemongrass—if you can't find the fresh or dried variety, simply omit the ingredient.

1 With a large sharp knife, slice the meat into very thin strips; set aside. Peel the shallots and garlic and finely chop. Then cut the hot chile crosswise into thin rings. Peel and finely grate the ginger. Squeeze the juice from the lime. Finely chop the white portion of the lemongrass, discarding the rest.

2 In a medium bowl, stir together the shallots, garlic, chile, ginger, lime juice, lemongrass, coriander, and soy sauce. Add the meat, then stir to combine. Set aside for 1 hour.

3 Meanwhile, place the grated coconut in a bowl with 2 cups of water and let soak for 15 minutes. Over a bowl, strain the coconut through a fine sieve, pressing with a spoon and squeezing with your hands to extract as much coconut milk as possible.

4 Cut the broccoli into florets; peel the stalks and thinly slice diagonally. Heat the oil in a wok over high heat. Add the meat; stir-fry for 2 minutes. Add the broccoli and coconut milk; bring to a boil. Reduce the heat and simmer for 7 minutes. Garnish with chopped cilantro leaves and serve.

Step 1

Step 2

Step 3

Preparation: 30 minutes
Marinating: 1 hour
Cooking: 10 minutes
Per serving: 527 cal; 33 g pro;
36 g fat; 23 g carb.

TYPICALLY THAI
Thai cuisine is well-known for its appetizing presentations of multidish meals, and this tradition of artistry extends beyond the kitchen. Handmade textiles and other arts and crafts also showcase the Thai flair for vibrant colors and fine detail.

COOKING TIPS

• To save time, use canned coconut milk instead of straining the juice yourself (Step 3).

• After working with chiles, wash your hands thoroughly. It's important to avoid touching your eyes and face—these strong peppers really sting!

SERVING TIPS

Your guests are certain to enjoy an appetizer of grilled shrimp with a savory soy dipping sauce.

Limeade, lemonade, jasmine tea, or beer will go nicely with this meal.

ℬEEFSTEAKS TERIYAKI

JAPAN

Perhaps the most popular sauce in Japan, teriyaki is a tangy blend of rice wine and soy sauce. Here, beef marinates and cooks in the sauce, which caramelizes into a beautiful glaze.

INGREDIENTS
(Serves 4)

- ¼ cup mirin or marsala
- ¼ cup soy sauce
- 4 filets mignons or boneless sirloin steaks (6 ounces each)
- 2 scallions
- 1 small carrot
- 2-inch piece fresh ginger
- 2 tablespoons oil

INGREDIENT TIP

Mirin is a strong, sweet rice wine used exclusively for cooking in Japanese cuisine. Look for it in Asian specialty-food stores. When grilled or sautéed, the wine caramelizes, giving meat and fish a delightful glaze. If you can't find mirin, use marsala, a fortified wine from Sicily.

1 In a resealable plastic bag, combine the mirin and soy sauce. Add the steaks and seal the bag. Marinate for 10 minutes. Trim the scallions, cut into 2-inch pieces, then thinly slice lengthwise. Place the scallions in a bowl of cold water and set aside.

2 Trim and peel the carrot. Place the wider end on a work surface and carefully carve several grooves along the length of the carrot. Slice crosswise; place in another bowl of cold water. Peel the ginger, cut into thin shreds and add to the carrot.

3 Heat 1 tablespoon of oil in a large skillet over high heat. Drain the carrot and ginger and add to the pan. Stir for 30 seconds, then transfer to a plate and keep warm.

4 Remove the meat from the marinade and add to the pan with the remaining 1 tablespoon oil. Cook the meat on each side for 2 minutes. Pour in the marinade and boil for 2 minutes, turning the meat twice. Transfer the steaks to a board, let rest for 5 minutes, then slice. Transfer to plates and pour the pan juices on top. Drain the scallions and place next to the meat along with the carrot and ginger.

Step 1

Step 2

Step 4

Preparation: 20 minutes
Cooking: 10 minutes
Per serving: 392 cal; 37 g pro; 20 g fat; 3 g carb.

TYPICALLY JAPANESE

Meat did not appear on a menu in Japan until the middle of the 19th century because most Japanese subscribed to a meatless Buddhist diet. In more recent years, Japanese cuisine has become famous for its excellent beef.

COOKING TIP

Take care to use steaks that are of uniform size and thickness—this ensures that they will cook evenly within the given amount of time. The times we've given are for rare steaks—for medium doneness, you'll need an additional 1-2 minutes.

SERVING TIPS

Steamed dumplings or an assortment of purchased sushi would make an excellent appetizer for the beef.

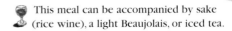

This meal can be accompanied by sake (rice wine), a light Beaujolais, or iced tea.

SERVING TIPS You can garnish the dish with thin strips of leek that have been chilled in ice water.

Offer green tea or rice wine, which can be gently heated for a warming winter's-night treat.

ZESTY MARINATED JAPANESE BEEF

JAPAN

This quick-cooking dish's delightful fragrance will make your mouth water. Shiitake mushrooms lend it a particularly Japanese accent—but regular white mushrooms also work well.

INGREDIENTS
(Serves 4)

- 1 pound beef tenderloin
- 2 teaspoons cornstarch
- ½ cup soy sauce
- ½ cup sake or dry sherry
- pinch of sugar
- 2 cups long-grain white rice
- 1 scallion
- 1 small leek
- 2 garlic cloves
- 8 ounces shiitake or white mushrooms
- 2 tablespoons peanut oil
- ½ cup beef broth
- 1 tablespoon sesame oil

INGREDIENT TIP

For a change from long-grain white rice, try sticky rice. It's wonderfully chewy and easy to eat with chopsticks. You can find it in Asian markets.

1 Thinly slice the beef. Place on paper towels and sprinkle with the cornstarch. In a medium bowl, mix the soy sauce, sake, and sugar. Add the meat and stir to mix well. Cover and let stand for 20 minutes.

2 Meanwhile, cook the rice according to package directions. Trim the scallion, thinly slice, and set aside. Trim the leek root and dark green portion. Rinse the white portion well and cut into thin slivers. Peel and mince the garlic. Thinly slice the mushrooms.

3 Heat the peanut oil in a wok or large skillet over high heat. Remove the meat from the marinade and add to the pan, reserving the marinade. Stir-fry for 1 minute. Add the garlic and mushrooms and stir-fry for 2 minutes. Add the leek, broth, and the reserved marinade. Bring to a simmer and continue to cook until thickened.

4 Turn off the heat, then stir in the sesame oil. Serve the meat and vegetables over the rice and sprinkle with the scallion.

Step 1

Step 1

Step 3

Preparation: 15 minutes
Marinating: 20 minutes
Cooking: 10 minutes
Per serving: 843 cal; 31 g pro; 37 g fat; 86 g carb.

TYPICALLY JAPANESE

In the garden as well as in the kitchen, the Japanese have made an art of harmonizing color and form. In Japan, garden design—and the floral decor in restaurants—changes throughout the year, capturing the beauty and spirit of each season.

BENGALI BEEF CURRY

INDIA

An aromatic array of seasonings—fresh ginger, garlic, cumin, coriander, thyme, cinnamon, and more—lend this dish the particular allure and flair of authentic curry.

INGREDIENTS
(Serves 4)

- 1½ pounds lean stew beef
- 4 tablespoons vegetable oil
- 4 garlic cloves
- 1 jalapeño chile
- salt and pepper
- 2 tablespoons lemon juice
- 2 medium onions
- 2-inch piece fresh ginger
- 2 teaspoons ground cumin
- 1 teaspoon ground coriander
- 1 teaspoon dried thyme
- 2 sticks (2-inch) cinnamon
- 3 bay leaves
- 1½ cups beef broth

INGREDIENT TIP

Cumin, a standard ingredient in most Indian curries, is available in large supermarkets and Middle Eastern specialty-foods stores.

1 Cut the beef into 1½-inch cubes. Heat 1 tablespoon oil in a large skillet and brown half the meat over high heat. Remove with a slotted spoon to a plate. Repeat with the remaining meat.

2 Peel the garlic. Mince half the jalapeño and cut the other half into rings. In a mortar, mash the garlic with the minced jalapeño, 1 teaspoon salt, ¼ teaspoon black pepper, and 1 tablespoon lemon juice. Peel the onions and ginger. Chop one onion. Cut the other into rings and separate the rings. Finely chop the ginger.

3 Heat 1 tablespoon oil in the skillet over medium heat and sauté the onion rings and jalapeño rings for 2 minutes. Remove and reserve. Add 1 tablespoon oil to the skillet and sauté the chopped onion and ginger for 5 minutes. Add the cumin, coriander, and thyme, and sauté for 1 minute. Add the meat, garlic paste, cinnamon, bay leaves, and broth; bring to a boil. Cover and simmer for 1 hour.

4 Add the onion and jalapeño rings and boil for 5 minutes to thicken the sauce. Remove the cinnamon and bay leaves.

Step 1

Step 2

Step 3

Preparation: 30 minutes
Cooking: 1 hour 10 minutes
Per serving: 422 cal; 35 g pro; 27 g fat; 9 g carb.

TYPICALLY BENGALI

Although many Bengali are Hindu, this dish was introduced to the region by Muslims. It is often prepared with lamb or goat and always with lots of onions.

COOKING TIPS

• For a milder flavor, remove the seeds and membranes from the jalapeño chile.

• While frying the onions, take particular care not to let them brown—the curry may take on a bitter taste.

SERVING TIPS

Offer Indian flatbreads, chutneys, and *raita* (yogurt with finely cubed cucumber) with this dish.

 Serve with a Gewürztraminer wine, beer, or Darjeeling tea.

ℳEATLOAF BURGERS

USA

The famed hamburger on a bun arrived with the first German immigrants to America. Here, a fried egg tops the seasoned meat filling for a unique variation on a national favorite.

INGREDIENTS

(Serves 4)

- 1 pound ground beef
- ¼ pound ground pork
- 1 small shallot
- ⅓ cup chopped parsley
- salt and pepper
- 2 tablespoons vegetable oil
- 2 hamburger buns
- 2 tablespoons butter
- 4 eggs

INGREDIENT TIP

Hamburger patties are usually made of ground beef chuck. We use a mixture of beef and pork, which enhances the flavor and texture. Be sure to cook through thoroughly. If you prefer, you can use all-beef patties.

1 Place the beef and pork in a medium bowl. Peel and finely dice the shallot, and add to the meat. Add the parsley, 1 teaspoon salt, and ½ teaspoon pepper. Lightly mix the ingredients with your hands.

2 Form the meat mixture into four 1-inch-thick patties, pressing the ingredients together just enough to insure that the burgers will not fall apart when fried.

3 Heat the oil in a large skillet over medium-high heat and cook the burgers for 4–5 minutes on each side, until browned and cooked through. Remove the burgers to a plate and cover with foil. Split the buns in half and toast lightly on each side.

4 Wipe the skillet with a paper towel, and melt the butter over medium heat. Fry the eggs to the desired doneness. Place each burger onto a bun and top with a fried egg.

Step 1

Step 2

Step 3

Preparation: 25 minutes
Cooking: 15 minutes
Per serving: 543 cal; 32 g pro; 40 g fat; 12 g carb.

TYPICALLY AMERICAN

Americans love hamburgers—we enjoy them at food stands, restaurants, and in our own homes. Of German origin, the hamburger was originally a fried patty of beef, topped with crispy onions. It wasn't until the 20th century that it was served on a soft bun.

COOKING TIPS

• The burgers should be between 1 and 1½ inches thick. Adjust the heat so the meat browns nicely but not too quickly before turning the patties to cook on the other side. That way they will be cooked through but still juicy on the inside.

• Keep the toasted buns and cooked burgers warm while frying the eggs.

SERVING TIPS

Popular accompaniments include roasted potatoes or french fries, pickles, and crisp lettuce.

 For refreshment, serve cold soft drinks, beer, or a California Pinot Noir.

CAJUN-STYLE BLACKENED STEAK

USA

INGREDIENTS
(Serves 4)

- 1 cucumber
- 1 yellow bell pepper
- 1 garlic clove
- 2 tomatoes
- 1 teaspoon sugar
- salt
- 4 teaspoons paprika
- 2 teaspoons dried thyme
- 1 teaspoon cayenne pepper
- ¼ teaspoon garlic powder
- 4 thick sirloin steaks (1½ pounds total)
- 1 cup thick plain yogurt
- ½ avocado
- a few lettuce leaves (such as chicory or red leaf)

INGREDIENT TIP

Thick, creamy whole milk yogurt is available in some markets, but if necessary, you can substitute low-fat yogurt.

Here, the meat is dipped in a mixture of piquant, Cajun-style seasonings, then seared without oil to produce the crisp, dark, tasty crust that makes these steaks irresistibly good.

1 Peel the cucumber, slice lengthwise, and remove the seeds. Cut it crosswise into thin slices and place in a medium bowl. Cut the bell pepper in half, remove seeds, and slice into strips. Peel and mince the garlic. Cube the tomatoes. Add the bell pepper, garlic, tomatoes, sugar, and ½ teaspoon salt to the cucumber. Mix well, cover, and refrigerate.

Step 1

2 Mix the paprika, thyme, cayenne, garlic powder, and a pinch of salt in a cup. Spread the mixture over the meat to coat.

3 Heat a large skillet over high heat until very hot. Add the steaks and cook for 5 minutes on each side, until the spicy crust becomes crisp and dark.

Step 2

4 Cut the steaks into slices and arrange on a plate with the tomato-cucumber salad. Place a dollop of yogurt on each salad. Peel the avocado and cut into slices. Place the avocado slices and lettuce leaves alongside the salad.

Step 4

Preparation: 40 minutes
Cooking: 10 minutes
Per serving: 487 cal; 37 g pro; 32 g fat; 14 g carb.

TYPICALLY CAJUN

Descendants of French immigrants to Louisiana from Canada, France, and the French West Indies are known as Cajuns. Their famous cuisine reflects the spirit of the culture—adventuresome yet modest, with just enough French joie de vivre.

COOKING TIPS

• Since the blackened steaks are fried without oil, it's best to use a heavy pan, such as a cast-iron skillet.

• Don't prepare the salad too far in advance—the salt draws water out of the cucumber, making it less crisp and fresh-tasting.

SERVING TIPS

As an appetizer, serve peeled boiled shrimp with a bold garlic mayonnaise dipping sauce.

A California Cabernet Sauvignon rounds out the effect. Iced tea is also a good beverage choice.

$\mathscr{S}$PICY BEEF, BEAN & VEGETABLE TACOS

MEXICO

This is a colorful, hearty meal that will lure family and friends to the table. Everyone loves crispy taco shells filled with savory seasoned meat, beans, and fresh vegetables.

INGREDIENTS
(Serves 4)

- 1 red onion
- 2 garlic cloves
- 1 tablespoon vegetable oil
- ¾ pound ground beef
- 1 jalapeño chile
- 2 tablespoons tomato paste
- 1 teaspoon ground coriander
- ½ teaspoon ground cumin
- salt and black pepper
- 4 small firm tomatoes
- 4 scallions
- 2 large ripe avocados
- 1 tablespoon fresh cilantro
- ¼ teaspoon cayenne pepper
- juice from 1 lime
- 1 can (8¾ ounces) kidney beans
- 12 taco shells
- 1 green bell pepper
- 1 cup shredded lettuce
- 1 cup grated cheddar cheese

1 Peel the onion and garlic. Cut the onion into rings and mince the garlic. Heat the oil in a large skillet over medium heat. Add the onion, garlic, and beef, and sauté for 5 minutes. Mince the jalapeño and add to the beef mixture. Stir in 1½ cups water, the tomato paste, coriander, cumin, 1 teaspoon salt, and ¼ teaspoon black pepper. Bring to a boil. Simmer over low heat for 20 minutes.

Step 1

2 Meanwhile, cut 2 tomatoes into wedges, remove the seeds, and set aside. For the salsa, seed and dice the remaining tomatoes and place in a medium bowl. Slice the scallions and add to the diced tomatoes.

Step 2

3 Halve the avocados; remove the pit and peel. Cut 1 avocado into cubes; add to the salsa. Add the cilantro, cayenne, ½ teaspoon salt, and the lime juice. Mix well.

4 Drain the beans, rinse, and stir into the beef. Cook for 10 minutes. Heat the taco shells (see Cooking Tip). Seed and cut the green pepper into strips. Cut the second avocado into slices. Fill each taco shell with lettuce and bell pepper, then meat, cheese and salsa. Garnish with avocado slices and tomato wedges. Pass the remaining salsa.

Step 3

Preparation: 20 minutes
Cooking: 35 minutes
Per serving: 889 cal; 32 g pro; 65 g fat; 49 g carb.

T Y P I C A L L Y   M E X I C A N
Mexican cooking is a blend of ethnic flavors and cultural traditions. This dish mixes native Mexican staple ingredients—tomatoes, chiles, beans, and corn tortillas—with beef and cheese, which were introduced to the cuisine by Spanish conquistadores in the 16th century.

COOKING TIP

To bring out their corn flavor, prepared taco shells must be heated in the oven or microwave. For the crispiest shells, heat in the oven, and use this trick to ensure that they keep their shape: Hang them over the bars of the oven rack.

SERVING TIPS

Guacamole, a dip made of pureed avocados and spices, is the perfect complement to tacos.

 Offer a refreshing ice-cold Corona or another Mexican beer with a wedge of lime.

SERVING TIPS Colorful Mexican-style rice and a tossed salad go very well with this dish.

Offer your guests a fruity white wine or sangria, a blend of wine, juices, soda water, and fresh fruit.

56

PORK MEDALLIONS VERACRUZ

MEXICO

These tender pork medallions are generously seasoned and pan-browned. Oranges, fresh cilantro, and cumin lend the dish its vibrant, characteristically Mexican flavor.

INGREDIENTS
(Serves 4)

- 1 pound pork tenderloin, trimmed
- 2 tablespoons all-purpose flour
- 2 tablespoons Dijon mustard
- ½ teaspoon ground cumin
- salt and pepper
- 1 medium orange
- ¼ cup dry white wine
- ¼ cup chicken broth
- 2 tablespoons vegetable oil
- 1 tablespoon chopped fresh cilantro

INGREDIENT TIP

The tiny leaves of cilantro look like parsley but have a different, licoricelike flavor. When it is cooked, the herb loses its color, so it should be added to the dish just before serving.

1 Cut the pork into ⅓-inch-thick slices. In a small bowl, whisk the flour, mustard, cumin, ½ teaspoon salt, and ¼ teaspoon pepper until blended.

2 Spread the mustard mixture evenly on one side of the pork slices. Squeeze the juice from the orange into another small bowl, and add the wine and chicken broth.

Step 1

3 Heat 1 tablespoon oil in a large skillet over medium-high heat. Place half of the pork slices in the pan, mustard-side down and brown for 2 minutes. Turn the slices over and brown for 2 minutes longer. Remove the slices to a plate, keep warm, and repeat with the remaining 1 tablespoon oil and pork.

Step 2

4 Add the orange juice mixture and a pinch of salt to the skillet. Bring to a boil over high heat, stirring to mix in the drippings and deglaze the pan.

5 Stir the chopped cilantro into the sauce and pour the sauce onto a platter. Top with the pork slices.

Step 2

Preparation: 30 minutes
Cooking: 10 minutes
Per serving: 241 cal; 25 g pro; 11 g fat; 6 g carb.

TYPICALLY MEXICAN

Citrus fruits became popular in Spain during the Middle Ages. The Spanish in turn introduced them to Mexico, where they were quickly incorporated into the country's cuisine.

TRADITIONAL BEEF FAJITAS

MEXICO

Your friends and family—especially kids—will enjoy creating their own fajitas: Pass around a platter of soft tortillas and serve the meat-and-vegetable filling and sour cream alongside.

INGREDIENTS
(Serves 4)

- 1 pound flank or round beefsteak, trimmed
- 2 onions
- 2 garlic cloves
- 1 *each* red and green bell peppers
- 1 jalapeño chile
- ½ teaspoon ground cumin
- ½ teaspoon ground coriander
- ¼ teaspoon ground cinnamon (optional)
- ⅛ teaspoon cayenne pepper
- 2 tablespoons tequila (optional)
- 1 tablespoon lime juice
- 8 flour tortillas
- 1 tablespoon vegetable oil
- ½ cup sour cream

INGREDIENT TIP

Wash your hands after you work with chiles. Until you do, avoid touching your eyes.

1 Slice the beef across the grain into thin strips and place in a medium bowl. Peel and cut each onion into 8 wedges and place in another medium bowl. Peel and mince the garlic and add to the onions. Seed and devein the bell peppers, slice into strips, and add to the onions. Seed, devein, and mince the jalapeño and place in a small bowl. Add the spices, tequila, and lime juice.

2 Heat the flour tortillas in a bamboo or other type steamer placed over boiling water. If using freshly made tortillas, keep them warm by wrapping in a foil packet.

3 While the tortillas steam, heat the oil in a large skillet over high heat and sauté the onions, bell peppers, and garlic for 3 minutes. Add the beef and sauté until just cooked, about 2 minutes. Add the jalapeño mixture and sauté for 2 minutes longer. Remove to a serving platter.

4 Serve the beef and vegetables with the tortillas and sour cream.

Step 1

Step 2

Step 3

Preparation: 25 minutes
Cooking: 10 minutes
Per serving: 542 cal; 32 g pro; 23 g fat; 51 g carb.

TYPICALLY MEXICAN

In Mexico, a meal without tortillas is almost inconceivable—the lists of fillings and side dishes are endless. The climate is favorable for the cultivation of wheat in Northern Mexico, where flour tortillas are almost always on the table. In Central and Southern Mexico, however, tortillas are made from corn flour.

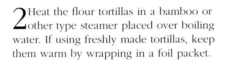

COOKING TIP

You can make your own flour tortillas. In a bowl, mix 1 cup flour and 1 teaspoon salt. Rub in 1 tablespoon margarine or lard. Stir in ⅔ cup water. Knead dough until smooth, about 5 minutes. Cover and let rest for 1 hour. Divide the dough in eighths; roll each piece out to a 7-inch round. Cook tortillas one at a time in a hot cast-iron skillet for 40–50 seconds, turning once.

SERVING TIPS

This dish goes very well with a salad of diced red bell peppers, kidney beans, and corn.

🍸 Offer your guests a cocktail, such as a tangy tequila sunrise or salt-rimmed margarita.

KITCHEN GLOSSARY

Here you will find many helpful tips to assist you in purchasing and using ingredients and in preparing the recipes.

AVOCADO

An avocado is ripe when you can easily press your finger into its skin. To ripen the fruit, place it in a paper bag for several days at room temperature. Once an avocado has been cut open, sprinkle with lemon juice to keep it from turning brown.

CILANTRO

The zesty green-leaved herb known as cilantro, or fresh coriander, plays an enormous role in Mexican and Asian cuisine. The seeds are prized as a spice, whole or ground, particularly in Southern Europe, North Africa, and the Near East.

COCONUT MILK

A creamy substance made from the white meat of the coconut. Pour boiling water over freshly grated or dried unsweetened coconut meat, allow it to soak for ½ hour, and then pour the liquid through a strainer, pressing on the solids. A canned version is available in specialty food markets.

LEMONGRASS

An important ingredient of Thai cooking: The hard green stems are discarded and only the lower white portion is used. These should be flattened first with a meat tenderizer, then cooked whole or sliced into thin, fine strips.

RICE VINEGAR

A mild vinegar made from rice wine with 3–4% acidity. A variety from Japan is colorless; those from China are pale amber, red, or black.

RICE WINE

In Japan, rice wine is called "sake"; in China it's "Shaoxing"—you can use either variety.

CUTS OF BEEF, PORK, LAMB, AND VEAL

Ground meat

For meatballs and burgers, use beef, pork, veal, or lamb. For the juiciest hamburgers, use ground beef chuck. It has the best lean-to-fat ratio.

Beef

One of the common cuts is the steak (sirloin, strip, T-bone). Others include roast, whole fillet, and top round. Leaner cuts are taken from the leg and neck.

Pork

A favorite cut for frying is the pork chop. There are many varieties of pork chop that you may choose depending on the type of dish you want to prepare. Loin chops are cut from the back. Medallions come from the tenderloin.

Lamb

Loin chops come from the hind quarter. Considerably more economical than the loin and just as delightfully tender is leg of lamb, which is sold whole or in steaks. Lamb shoulder is also relatively inexpensive and offers good kabob and stew meat.

Veal

Rib chops are taken from the forequarter below the neck, while the loin, or loin chops, are cut from the front part of the hind quarter. Cutlets, or scallops, come from the top, bottom, or eye round of the leg.

Both are sold in well-stocked markets and keep for a long time in the refrigerator. There is also a sweet Japanese rice wine called mirin. Paired with soy sauce, it makes a simple, delicious Japanese-style marinade for meat. It's also used as a seasoning for vegetables and in salad dressings.

SESAME OIL

Sesame oil is a golden yellow or dark amber seasoning oil produced from the toasted seeds of the sesame plant. It tastes slightly nutty and is sprinkled on the dish just before serving.

SOY SAUCE

A fermented condiment made from boiled soy beans, salt, and roasted wheat or barley, soy sauces range in color from light to dark and are among the fundamental ingredients of Asian cuisine.

TOMATOES

Fresh plum tomatoes are great for cooking since they're flavorful and firm; they won't break down into mush. They're also available year-round nowadays. You can substitute canned Italian peeled tomatoes if you can't find fresh.

PREPARATION AND COOKING

Cutting meat
If you're cutting meat before cooking, slice against the grain—it will keep tender. Meat that's sliced with the grain is tougher and difficult to chew. This is particularly true for fillets or loin, whether of beef, pork, or veal. A sharp knife will make the task easier.

Marinating
Meat can be soaked in a special marinade before cooking. The addition of spices, herbs, and vegetables contributes flavor. Vinegar, wine, or lemon juice tenderizes and oil prevents the meat from drying out.

Browning
Stovetop meat is usually browned on all sides over a high heat in the first stages of cooking. This method caramelizes the exterior of the meat and gives it a more intense flavor.

Braising
Meat is first browned on all sides and then gently simmered—either covered or uncovered—in a small amount of liquid, such as broth, wine, beer, juice, or water.

Breading
Coating meat with a layer of egg and bread crumbs and then cooking it in hot oil creates a crispy crust that helps seal in the meat's juices. It also provides a crunchy textural contrast to the tender meat.

Stir-frying
Here, the ingredients (meats, vegetables) are cut into small pieces and cooked briefly over very high heat; a spatula or wooden spoon is used to stir constantly. After a short time, sauces are added.

WOK

A large, bowl-shaped metal pan often used in Asian cuisine. The wok is particularly suited for stir-frying, since the ingredients can be cooked quickly and carefully. Woks come in a variety of stovetop and electric designs, and the latter come with built-in heating elements for cooking at tableside.

ℳENU SUGGESTIONS

The following menu combinations should serve as an inspiration for you when you want to surprise your friends or family with a multicourse international meal.

ITALY

STEAK ALLA PIZZAIOLA
P. 6
Steamed Artichokes
Hazelnut Biscotti
— ◆ —

VEAL SALTIMBOCCA P. 8
Salad of Warm
Asparagus
Tiramisu
— ◆ —

**FLORENTINE MEDALLIONS
OF PORK** P. 10
*Spaghetti with
Tomato-Basil Sauce
Lemon Sorbet*
— ◆ —

SPAIN

ANDALUSIAN PORK P. 12
*Marinated Sweet
Red Peppers
Poached Apricots*
— ◆ —

GREECE

LAMB AVGOLEMONO P. 14
*Rice with Eggplant
Honeyed Fresh Figs and
Ice Cream*
— ◆ —

FRANCE

**STEAK WITH
SEASONED BUTTERS** P. 18
*French Green
Beans Almondine
Glazed Apple Tart*
— ◆ —

STEAK AU POIVRE P. 20
*Tomato-Roquefort
Gratin
Chocolate Ice Cream*
— ◆ —

**NORMAN
PORK CUTLETS** P. 22
*Ratatouille
Poached Pears with
Chocolate Sauce*
— ◆ —

VEAL-AND-MUSHROOM
ROULADES P. 24
*Carrot and Watercress Salad
Strawberry Tart*
— ◆ —

GERMANY

**SAVORY CROQUETTES
WITH MUSHROOM SAUCE**
P. 26
*Sauteed Broccoli
and Cauliflower
Fresh Fruit Salad*
— ◆ —

SWITZERLAND

**VEAL SCALLOPS IN
RASPBERRY-CREAM SAUCE**
P. 28
*Wild Mushroom Risotto
Cherry Compote with
Wafer Cookies*
— ◆ —

AUSTRIA

**CLASSIC WIENER
SCHNITZEL** P. 30
*Vegetable Soup
Marinated Strawberries*

RUSSIA

BEEF STROGANOFF P. 32
*Warm Peas with
Butter and Mint
Pecan Shortbread*

—◆—

CHINA

**STIR-FRIED BEEF
& VEGETABLES** P. 36
*Egg Drop Soup
Sliced Mango and
Coconut*

—◆—

**PORK WITH
SPRING ONIONS** P. 38
*Egg Rolls
Litchis with
Ice Cream*

—◆—

**TANGY CANTONESE
PORK** P. 40
*Broccoli with
Garlic Sauce
Fortune Cookies*

—◆—

THAILAND

**CURRIED BEEF AND
BROCCOLI** P. 42
*Gingered
Shrimp Cocktail
Mango and Coconut
Mousse*

—◆—

JAPAN

BEEFSTEAKS TERIYAKI
P. 44
*Miso Soup
Ginger Pound Cake*

—◆—

**ZESTY MARINATED
JAPANESE BEEF** P. 46
*Shredded
Vegetable Slaw
Melon Salad*

—◆—

INDIA

**BENGALI BEEF
CURRY** P. 48
*Lentil Salad
Fruited
Rice Pudding*

—◆—

USA

**MEATLOAF
BURGERS** P. 50
*Tossed Green Salad
Hot Fudge Sundaes*

—◆—

CAJUN-STYLE
BLACKENED STEAK P. 52
*Corn Chowder
Pecan Pie*

—◆—

MEXICO

**SPICY BEEF, BEAN,
AND VEGETABLE
TACOS** P. 54
*Cucumber Salad
Banana-Pineapple
Sundaes*

—◆—

**PORK MEDALLIONS
VERACRUZ** P. 56
*Mushroom Quesadillas
Almond Flan*

—◆—

**TRADITIONAL
BEEF FAJITAS** P. 58
*Cool Avocado-
Tomato Soup
Mexican Chocolate
Cake*

—◆—

ℛECIPE INDEX

Photo Credits

Book cover and recipe photos:
©International Masters Publishers AB
Michael Brauner, Eising Food Photography, Dorothee Gödert, Neil Mersh, Peter Rees
Agency photographs:
Introduction: IFA Bilderteam: Bürgel, page 4, upper left; Gottschalk, page 4, lower left.
Cephas: Boreham, page 4/5, middle. Look: Martini, page 5, lower right.
Tony Stone: Beer, page 5, upper right.
Photos for the 'Typically' sections: A–Z Botanical Collection: Svensson, page 27.
Bavaria: Kanus, page 33; Viesti, page 57.
Focus: Müller-Elsner, page 22; Robert Harding: pages 6, 30.
Image Bank: Ge Pen, page 40; Knessel, page 18; Sumi Nori, page 47; Sund, page 36.
Impact: Cole, page 50; Good, page 39; Henley, pages 10, 14; Parkin, page 42; Roberts, page 24.
Helga Lade: Hornback, page 12. Look: Heeb, pages 19, 20.
Tony Stone: Hiser, page 54; Murphy, page 58.
Telegraph Colour Library: Grandadam, page 52. ZEFA: page 28; Damm, page 8.

© MCMXCVIII International Masters Publishers AB.
Recipes of the World ™ IMP AB,
produced by IMP Inc. under license.
All rights reserved. No part of this book may be
reproduced in any form or by any means without
the prior written permission of the publisher.
Printed in Italy.

ISBN 1-886614-80-6